A CLOTH OF FINE GOLD

POEMS OF THE INNER JOURNEY

DOROTHY WALTERS

Cover design and cover art by N. M. Rai

Other books by this author:

"Marrow of Flame, Poems of the Spiritual Journey"
(Hohm Press)

"Unmasking the Rose, A Record of a Kundalini
Initiation" (orig. Hampton Roads, now available
from Amazon or dorothywalters2@sbcglobal.net)

ISBN   978-1-4357-5776-9

This volume is dedicated to all those who know the
joy of the Beloved Within,
and to all those who seek the way,
and with special thanks to
Naga Moon Rai, who held the light aloft to guide me
on my creative path; Gail Thompson, long time
friend and supporter; and Karen Lester, constant
joy and inspiration, all of whom shared generously
of their knowledge and encouragement as
this project went forward.

Preface

These poems speak in many voices. Some are clearly of an overtly "spiritual" nature, and the debt to Rumi and other early writers such as Kabir and Mirabai will be obvious. Others are more secular in tone (poems on contemporary poets and artists, as well as nature), and still others are downright oracular, as if they were written by ancient priests or prophets. We poets take whatever gifts may come.

But all are serious in their way, and all are intended as offerings which give us a larger perspective on how it is possible to live, even to experience rapture itself, in a world where the divine nexus so often seems to be broken.

As for the obviously sacred verses, they unabashedly allude to the connection of human and divine without trying to name the latter or present a fixed belief system. Sometimes the poet even uses the word "god," but note the term bears no capital. In these passages, I am not speaking of the old god, the thundering patriarch who drove our ancestors near mad with his commandments and interdictions and who even today finds his followers. I am speaking of that other, softer, more hidden reality, who led Rumi to the sweet secrets of his poems, who met St. John in the darkness of night where they consummated their sacred love tryst, who danced with Mirabai on the roads. This "god" is, of course, also the goddess, for she is beyond gender. She is ultimate expression—the divine presence, the undeniable essence, the pulsating stream of love which informs everything that is, in blessing and joy when we open our hearts sufficiently.

All of us yearn for this holy embrace, to know more intimately the hidden mystery which hovers near. Sometimes we catch glimpses through the door, taste a sip of something a bit ambrosial, smell a whiff of some indefinable perfume. Traces of the Beloved.

At times, however, the transition is more abrupt. An unexpected event, a surprising occurrence triggers an awakening beyond all we have known before. Katherine Anne Porter called such pivotal encounters "the moment which changes everything." Some years ago I experienced such a moment. For me, it occurred through what is called spontaneous Kundalini awakening, and its consequences have rippled through and shaped my life ever since. It was then that I discovered that the Beloved (the term which mystics so frequently use to express the Divine Presence) was not a metaphor, but a reality, a felt feeling in the blood, and a discovery convincing beyond all textbooks or words.

Union with the Inner Beloved may involve states of rapture unlike anything we experience in our ordinary life. The awakened energies are often quite sensuous in tone, though they are markedly distinct from sexual experiences. They can be intense or gentle and soft, depending on the circumstances. In the early stages, they can be quite dramatic, as the many feeling centers of the body open. As time passes, the sensations diminish, and ultimately they are more like light playing through the body or perhaps the echo from a peal of distant mountain thunder. The language which poets traditionally use to describe these profound episodes is that of human love. Some suggest that such experience is the end and goal of all spiritual striving, final embrace by Infinite Love.

As all mystics and seekers know, the spiritual journey (like life itself) does not always advance in a fixed, logical progression of say, longing, preparation, and final union. Rather, it shifts back and forth, oscillates between yearning and apparent arrival, often to lead once more to new beginnings and repeated struggle. So with these poems, for they mirror how things really are on the long inward journey.

This book contains both poems of the heart and verses of the mind, for both are needed if we are to discover the resolution we are seeking. This fusion of rapture and thoughtfulness will, I think, bring us to the next stage of our ongoing evolution of consciousness, and transform us and our world.

June, 2008/ San Francisco

CONTENTS

Three: And Then She Bared Her
        Naked Breast: Poets,
            Seagulls, and Trees

A CLOTH OF FINE GOLD

You may think
that first lit flame
was the ultimate blaze,
the holy fire revealed.

What do you know
of furnaces?
This is a sun that returns
again and again, refining, igniting,
pouring your spirit
through a cloth of delicate gold
until all dross is taken
and you are sweet as
clarified butter
in god/the goddess' mouth.

ONE

IN THE CAVES BETWEEN THE DESERT DUNES

UNTIL EVEN THE ANGELS

What the heart wants
is to follow its true passion,
to lie down with it
near the reeds beside
the river,
to devour it in the caves
between the desert dunes,
to sing its notes
into the morning sky
until even the angels
wake up
and take notice
and look around
for their beloved.

A LANGUAGE YOU ONCE KNEW

There will be an invitation.
It will not come tied in ribbons
nor a message streaming down
from the sky.

There will be no Roman candles
sizzling
nor brilliant colors
exploding overhead.

Instead there will be a soft
whisper
in your ear,
something in a language
you once knew
and are trying to learn again.

In order to hear it,
you will need to
put down all your packages,
stop everything you are doing
and stand very still
then wait. . .
until something stirs inside.

THE VISITORS

Some let the angels
come into their house
like guests dropping by
for a visit,
some keep the door
locked against unwelcome intruders,
all windows tightly closed.

I say, let them enter
through every opening and aperture,
with wings spread wide
in billowing light,
faces radiant with love,
chanting their hymns
of transcendence and joy.

Let us listen
in full attention,
lifting our eyes
now and again
to behold, briefly,
this bewildering beauty,
this dazzlement of revelation.

And, should they leave,
let us savor
the scent which lingers in the room,
the single feather
we clasp in our hand.

BE PREPARED TO SWELTER

If you want to go there,
check your boots and your
water bottle carefully.
Find the map
that the old one gave you
so long ago
and do your best to
follow it,
though often
you will make the wrong turn,
go astray.

Be prepared to swelter
under many suns,
drown
in countless rivers.

You will be shipwrecked many times,
or else burnt to cinder,
dust to dust.

You will meet strange winged creatures
who have no names,
beings descending
from the sky
or rising up like cloud specters
from below.

They will tell you
how to continue,
what paths to follow,
but check carefully
what they say.

Sometimes you will fall
into canyons or caves,
and will not know
how to get out
until you see a
a faint light coming
from a crack or crevice,
lit wings beckoning.
.

When you at last arrive,
you may not remember
who you are,
what you were seeking,
why you came.

It will not matter.

Now only silence will do.

TASTING THE LIGHT

It will arrive suddenly,
when you are unaware.

It will come over you swiftly,
lightning flash
across a large surface of stone.

After everything has melted,
there will be the taste
of bronze and honeyed fruit,
burnt cinnamon,
something blue and electric in the air.

TAKEN

First, you must let your heart
be broken open
in a way you have never
felt before, cannot imagine.

You will
not know if what you are feeling
is anguish or joy,
something predestined
or merely old wounds
flowing once more,
reminders of all that is
unfinished in your life.

Something will flood into
your chest
like air sweetened by
desert honeysuckle,
love that is too strong.

You will stand there,
very still,
not seeing what this is.
Later, you will not remember
any of this
until the next time
when you will say,
yes, yes, I have known this before,
it has come again,
just as your lids close shut
again.

ONCE MORE

Once more,
I've been
summoned.

But I'm
not complaining.

I don't care
if you leap
from a plane
or jump
from your horse
and tackle me
on the Mongolian steppes,
or come by
strumming a guitar
and scattering rose petals.

Anything will do.
Just don't leave.

WHAT IS IT?

Not a sexual explosion
rocking the flesh.

Nor a spasm of longing
triggering the blood.

More like perfume
suffusing a room
filled with daffodils.

Or the barely heard sound
of a distant wind chime
resonating all your bones
to bliss.

HOLY FIRE

Some love like
packed volcanoes exploding,
ash and fire
spewing over mountains and shores
igniting everything in their path,
as if all history,
stretched to the edge,
were returning
in a river
of hot remembrance,
a blaze
of flowing passion and grief,

Fields turn into lakes of flame
devouring air, swallowing sky.
Earth surges in streams of
blood and clay,
and trees are sudden torches,
beacons signaling
distant heaven.

Other loves are like soft candles
that spread their glow
into the curtained corners of the house,
hands of light
soothing the darkness,
caressing the quiet
awake.

Who is to say
which is god?

CARVING US INTO CONSTANT LOVE

Do you know how many times
I have opened my body to Yours,
how often I have become
whatever it is You are.

I never know just when
You will arrive,
how You are going to look
that day.

Sometimes you are Shiva,
tendrils flaming
ever dancing to keep the world alive.

Sometimes that Buddha
who lives in my front room,
wise master,
vessel of compassion,
container of sensuous joy.

Yesterday You were
just an image
on a temple wall,
some long vanished holy man or woman
with an inviting smile,
no one I had heard of
before.

The form does not matter.
only that you have come
once more.

THE ANATOMY OF BLISS

No one knows why.
It could be anything,
a sudden shift in the atmosphere,
a rush of hormones,
the cells sparking off
one another's memories,
sharing secrets from
their own private past,
underground network of nerves

I can't unravel
this speech,
translate its phonemes
into anything meaningful,
recognizable, clear.

This is why I have abandoned
spokenness,
foresworn the hidden syllables
of desire.

I just let this whatever it is
play over me,
lead me to recognition
like a primal self
moving into dream state,
or else a wanton child
toying with its
mother's breast.

THE TRUTH SEEKERS

I am trampling over every wisdom
just to kiss the face of love.
Eric Ashford

Nobody told us how to think
or what to believe.
Or if they tried, we didn't listen,
busy with inner signals.

When we traveled,
we went our own way:
instead of compasses
we would simply sniff the air
and set our own course,
finding direction
like lost animals returning home.

Sometimes we went whistling along
with our hands in our pockets.
Sometimes we stumbled
over rock and rough clay,
falling forward to our knees,
bruising our hands.

But we always got up
and started again, cheerful,
knowing that
what we were looking for
was waiting up ahead,
shining and beautiful,
just as we had always pictured.

LIGHT OF A DIFFERENT FREQUENCY

They call it the ascending.
The soul divesting itself
of all the nonessentials
like a pilot desperately
throwing things overboard
trying to keep the plane aloft
in the storm,
or a wagon made lighter
as it struggles to make it
over the next steep hill.

It is laborious work.
It takes years or lifetimes
of effort.
It comes little by little,
the tiny increments of joy,
the ongoing intervals
of pain.

Always there is a polishing,
a honing.
A smoothing away of the
flaws,
the imperfections.

Then something grows lighter
within.
Shift to a higher register.
Light of a different frequency.
Pulsations flowing like light
or breath.
Heart crying its rapture,
silence like pain.
Who can find words

for this constantly moving
upward, this always being lifted
to a higher plateau,
where the blood grows thinner,
the atmosphere
ever more refined.

AT MIDNIGHT

To do this
you must surrender
all the advice which
was planted in you
by your grandmother,
your ancient aunt,
the old men by the fire.

You must give up
your convictions
of right and wrong,
notions of the possible and
the unattainable.

You must breathe deep,
drink bitter herbs,
put a talisman
beneath your pillow.

At midnight,
when you are neither
waking or sleeping,
they will come for you,
arriving in sledges
or else in fleets
of wheeled airy transports.

You will not know them,
but you will recognize their voices
speaking a language
you cannot comprehend.

Be ready to go,
spring out from your resting place,
don't stop to
put on your shoes
or check the fire
or even scribble a note of farewell.

THE OFFERING

Every cell, every bit
of bone, each atom of flesh
or feather of hair,
the soft muscle
which covers the heart—

all caught in
a final dissolution,
this ultimate embrace.

TWO

AFTER THE LIGHTNING FLASH

OF JOY

STRANDED

After the lightning flash of joy,
the startled one awakes
amidst the smoldering ashes
of her former self
and wonders where she is
and how she came to be
in this curious realm,
its dreamlike features and wavering shapes.

And so she longs for home:
familiar place of morning tea,
walks among the garden paths in spring,
night birds welcoming,
that domain where each thing looks and sounds
each day almost the same
as it did the day before,
or even years ago.

But in that fated moment of light
the boundaries sprang:
celestial tones,
the sudden tongue of love
traveling upward
to some breathless union
with the utterly unseen,
instant,
as when the universe itself flared forth
from that first packed bead of darkness
to make itself anew.

Now you must wonder where you are
and who you have become.
As if finitude itself had been unstrung,
and you, dazed voyager,
spin through endless space
traveling ever toward or else away
from something you can't quite see,
part of a larger plan,
or captive of your own
swollen dreams,
delirious vessel no longer suited
for that lost, half-remembered world,
and yet not ready
for that to come.

THE AWAKENING

After the angel came,
she more and more discovered
she had strange powers.

Things began to look different,
change appearance,
as when the cat
seemed cradled
in a brilliant colored egg
and its energies
flew upward
from its head.

Sometimes she felt waves
of sensuous feeling
flow through her body,
what they call ecstasy
when it happens
to a saint.

Other times
she wept
for no reason.

When she wanted to turn on
the t. v. or
make the screen brighter
or dimmer,
she simply pointed her finger
in that direction
and it complied.

One morning
all the clocks in the house
stopped at the same time
for no known reason.

Then she saw a ray extend
from her hand to the wall
and bounce back again.

If she wanted to summon
her husband
from the outdoors to make love,
she sent him a mental message
and he would appear.

Once she saw a map of
the universe
glowing on her husband's back
as he lay sleeping
beside her in bed
but she never told him
what she saw.

ALWAYS, THE TURNING

Yes, I know how it is
to go with uncertain feet,
a burden which grows
heavier
with each step.

I too have felt the silence
fall through the thickening air,
dark currents to carry you
into foreboding channels.

Always, there is the turning,
light descending
into darkness,
the constant reversal
of the poles.

The other face of love.

WE WAKE AND WONDER

On days like today
we wake and wonder
how we will manage
to enter this arriving hour,
another cycle
of the familiar wheel.

Like Rilke,
we ask,
who among the heavenly choir
would hear us if we cry?

We rise and turn the furnace up
to take away the morning chill.

In the kitchen
we stir about a bit,
set the teakettle on the stove
and wait for its cheering note,
reminder that this, like any day,
will come but once,
its gifts subtle and clear,
locked in time,
our time,
here in this unlikely
sequence,
where we are
witness and field,
ourselves the momentary opening
between the worlds
of sun and mist.

LIKE A PRIVATE SHOWING

You went before me.
I keep running over your
faces, like a private showing
of a film, an exhibit of old photos
in a small gallery.
I wasn't ready.

See, I have this new poem
of Rilke which I just
discovered--
I wanted to show it to you,
tell you what it meant to me,
get your impressions.

You taught me so much.
Gave so much of your beauty.
How can I bear it . . .
you were that slender boy
standing at the street corner
near campus
waiting to cross
(a man, actually)
in your brilliant green suede jacket,
your flaming hair,
image permanently etched
on my mind.

And you--the one I
happened to catch sight of
that day as you were
teaching your class--
when I saw you there
so utterly in command

(you could have inspired multitudes)
I caught my breath,
felt myself shoved backward
as if from a blow.
I knew you were someone to be reckoned with,
a presence, a poet,
a being destined for higher things
like Yeats (your passion)
or Maude Gonne (his)--
your voice still whispers in my ear
almost like a seduction.

How could you and the others
go so soon,
leave me here to contemplate
how it is
to walk through the streets
of this strange city
and not see anyone
you know,
to sit alone in the corner
of the cafe
over your opened book.

The night here
has a voice of its own,
the days grow long
even as the sun pales
and the mist deepens.

A HINGE IN TIME

And then there was the pain,
so vast it was like
a hinge in time,
an antediluvian landscape
where memories burned the breath
of all that moved
scalded the restless hours,
kept us quivering
and still.

There were no recipes
or ancient nostrums to heal, potions
or sages to dispense counsel,
our agony kept us burrowing
ever deeper
into the crevasses of our soul
seeking answers.

Which did not come.
Until at last
we made
final surrender,
leapt into the abyss
of waiting darkness,
gave up trying to know or fathom
with our riddled minds,
relinquished everything,
even the last scattered particles
of who we were.
And then the sweetness
moved again.

BROKEBACK MOUNTAIN

(Brokeback Mountain is the name of a movie which
played in 2006. It tells the story of two lovers, male
cowboys, who fell in love one summer and later were
separated through the condemnations of a rejecting
society.)

I keep telling myself
it was only a movie,
but no,
that grief has taken over my soul,
moved in like a thief
and now inhabits
the whole house,
this house with dark ribbons
on the door.

Old wounds throbbing once again,
old sorrows weeping
like statues in a burial ground.

They came together
like two lightning clouds clashing,
touched by a rod.

A brief flash sweeping across
the granite stones.
Momentary roar
of thunder,
the beast springing . . .

Then silence everywhere.

THE PILGRIM'S SONG

If you ask me about holy longing
I can tell you how it is to go on
for lifetimes with hands
holding nothing
but a begging bowl
filled with regret
and a thin film of desire,
waiting for rain.

STRAWBERRIES RIPE

Whatever you have done in this world,
whether you carried
each day heavily,
like a plate of fish on which
only the skeleton and scales remain,
bound for the discard
almost
before the meal has begun,
or whether
you awoke joyously,
crying,
yes, this is the day
the orchard is ready,
the strawberries
ripe for plucking—
whichever way
you greeted your life,
put on it your special stamp,
that day will remain forever,
part of the great mind,
the memory of how it is
to live on this earth,
with its many
hollows and hills,
its constant rippling
up and down
across the changing surfaces,
carrying us always
to the next destination,
another arrival.

THE ASCENT

Yes, there is a mountain.

Yes, you are on it,
struggling upward,
stumbling over boulder
and rock.

There are others climbing with you.
Sometimes you nod
to one another,
sometimes you move in silence.

Occasionally, the clouds break open,
reveal a hazy glory up ahead,
something green and golden,
fairy tale kingdom from a child's
picture book.

Meanwhile, heavy legs lifting
again and again,
stone upon stone layering
the rising trail.
You think there must be an easier way,
a shortcut or secret tunnel.
Someone will surely
come for you.

But if you imagine you are, one day,
going to be lifted up by an angel
and whisked to the top once more,
and there be fitted with shining golden wings
to carry you to unseen edens yet beyond,
no, that will not happen.

Your path is here,
plodding over hard rubble
and scree
in a light that is failing,
an atmosphere that
ever thins.

Sometimes you're not sure
there is a mountain.
If you are there, moving upward,
toward some intended destination,
some longed for journey's end.

AND EVEN THEN

And if, say, one day
you reach the summit of the holy mount
and are there shattered utterly by light,
even then,
you must go on
not like a saint spiraling upward,
delicate feet barely tracing
invisible arcs of air,
but back once more
at the granite foot,
the rubbled start of it all
where you join again the struggling band,
pilgrims climbing together
on hands and rock-torn knees.

WHAT IF

What if it is given to us
not to know, but to feel constantly
those currents of love and agony
which flow unceasingly
through us, through the world,
thrilling the trees
with their bent boughs,
caressing the waves torn by their own
incessant pummeling
against the shore,
even the birds
when they are not here.

What if we can never unravel
the mystery of the eye
following the shimmering beam to
the lover's eye,
the lip seeking the lip,
the invalid crying
alone.

What if we can uncover nothing
beyond this terrible knowing,
this anguished rapture?

A DEEPER INTENSITY

We must be still and still moving
Into another intensity
For a further union, a deeper communion.
T. S. Eliot

Yes, that's it . . .
a deeper intensity,
a going into
and beyond,
a discovery against which
the others pale
the moment which carries us
into a realm
prefigured only
in our dreams.

And each return
brings new wonder,
unexpected delight,
exhilaration carried
to its furthest limit,
the life turning
on its own axis,
molecule linked
to eternity.

STILL, I AM SHAMELESS

Who am I
to say things about Love?

Even on days like today
when memory alone
must suffice. . .

Sometimes it is enough
just to think
of all that has happened
between us,
midnight meetings
in broad daylight,
love strokes
from invisible hands.

I no longer grieve
for the lost embrace,
but wait for the
certain return,
the knock at the window
sure to come.

Still, I am shameless
in my need,
like an aging mistress
who fingers old ribbons
and pearls
for reassurance.

Even god has moments of longing.

MEDITATION

I am not a Buddhist
nor am I a yogi.

My robe has no
special emblem
or design.

My Great Teacher
is Silence.

I sit here now
listening.

THE ANCIENT TAOIST ABANDONS HIS
LIBRARY

Why should I keep reading
more and more volumes,
endless stacks mounting
ever skyward?
Words piled on words
revealing less and less?
Will they become a ladder to heaven?

For what reason should I cling
to these wordy prescriptions,
drawn out expositions
of the manifestly obvious?

I have met them all,
the three precepts,
the seven pillars,
the eleven guiding principles.
Yin and yang,
receptive and active,
lover and beloved--
these simple pairs encompass the whole.
Tell me, can you draw
a line around god?

God/goddess in the soul dances
and I too make my turns,
embrace my joy.

I think I will go out
into the night garden
and wander among the moon flowers
floating among the rivered buds.

NO MATTER HOW

A puzzle without an answer,
a sleeve that unravels
before the garment is done.

No matter how we put it together
it is never complete.
These tattered edges,
these ragged selvages,
this is what we have,
our scant materials
for sewing this robe of truth.

IN THE HAWK'S EYE

God, I think,
is both fluidity and fixation,
still point and moving wheel.
Particle and wave.

Like that giant hawk we saw
high above the ocean's cliff,
riding the wind, hanging so still
we thought it was a toy,
mechanical design
made to astonish and amuse
until we noticed
its relentless gaze
that spared nothing below
and then it took off
with a determined swoop
heading out over the waters
to the horizon's fold.

Likewise, some part of god
dances, dances,
keeping the vast currents
of the world alive,
while the immutable other
rests at ease
an abstracted principle
at the midpoint of all,
observer and thing seen,
seeker and goal,
reflecting each movement
in his unwavering eye.

.NOT A THOUSAND PROSTRATIONS
(Inspired by Mary Oliver)

1.

You do not have to
change your name
in order for god
to love you.

You are not required to rise
at a certain hour
nor wear a robe
of a prescribed color
because that's what
the others have chosen to do.

You needn't make
the thousand prostrations
nor circumnavigate the holy mountain
a hundred times
nor dwell on an image
of an imaginary form
until you think
that being is who you are.

But you must wash your heart again and again
in the pure fountain where sanctity dwells.

You must cleanse your spirit many times over
in the cauldrons of love.

Only love, my friend,
can take you there.
Only the fiercest seekers
find the way.

2.

Still no one requires
that you be perfect,
that you turn away from the world
and live in a dark cavern
like a saint preparing to ascend.
Or that you stripe you back
with lashes, expiation
for the world's gross blunders,
your own hidden miscalculations.

It isn't even necessary
to be fully informed,
to know all about everything,
or even a single thing,
for that matter.

What is important
is to be who you are,
to come ahead
with your small allotment of wisdom
garnered through the years,
your residue of compassion
eager to be shared.

If you paused to feed the pigeons
in the park one day,
that will count for you.
If you saw what was happening
to the forest
or spoke out against the sullying
of the noble sea,
heard the cry of the children
or the rising drums of war

and raised your voice in protest,
that will suffice.

Meanwhile,
dance as naked as you can.
Breathe your secret breath.
Let the world's warm currents
enter your body,
show you the way.

I CANNOT TELL YOU

I do not know
if god
is a thing
or a process,
or a being
or a presence.

I cannot tell you
how the world
was constructed,
or when it began
or by whom.

I cannot unravel
the tables of meaning,
the diagrams
and the scales of comparison,
the charts and the long explanations
of everything
that has ever been.

What I know is this:
this moment,
this kiss,
this infinite longing,
endless loving and being loved
by no one
who has a name
in a place
that does not exist.

THE PANTHER IN THE SOUL

Aloof as a planet, clad in iridescent orange,
you strode across my dream
in brilliant unconcern--
that radiant hue
against its field of gray
told me you were not of this world,
that you had somehow wandered into mine,
that I was lucky to get this furtive glimpse
of the profoundly Other.

Were you indeed my spirit guide,
glittering totem beast finally come round
to let me see your ancient face,
lead me onward
after all these years?

Or were you merely some mythic
creature out on a
casual astral stroll
who happened by chance
to come my way?

I must practice walking
with greater intent,
move with more supple majesty,
summon a stronger sense of who I am.

REFINING THE ESSENTIALS

All right, then,
give me a cave.

I'm sure I could learn
to live there,
find my way to god.

Dried figs, a few thistles and thorns,
the occasional gift
of meal.
Constant whispered prayers.
What else is needed?

The heat, glistening like shaken mercury
by day,
the moon winking suggestively at night,
brazen old strumpet, beckoning.

Sometimes an owl song
in the distance.
Sometimes a desert bird
or the cry of a doomed animal.

Mostly just silence,
the wind speaking
to itself,
the rain crooning
its ancient unknowable song.

THREE

AND THEN SHE BARED HER NAKED BREAST: POETS, SEAGULLS AND TREES

THE SEA GULLS

Huddled in clusters
along the small lake's shore,
they rose and took flight
like a white rose opening
swiftly in air;
together they swooped over,
then, closing again,
became a ball of flame
which exploded and fell
earthward on the distant rim,
like a fireworks shattering
in phosphorescent glee,
spiraling brilliance,
feathered light.

IN THE BOTANICAL GARDENS

1.

WHEN NAKED TO NAKED GOES

I have come here
to see you naked.
To witness your hidden
geometry of passion
laid bare, here,
in this winter's time.

The brilliant hues of summer
have vanished—
the shimmering pinks
and blazing blood orange reds
the boisterous yellows
and gleaming peacock blues—

all have faded, melted into
the earth's pale mouth,
leaving behind this stark revelation,
the denuded underpinnings of desire.

I pause and marvel
at this muted bliss,
unclothed conspiracy of all
things which remain
and rise in joy.

Yeats said truth arrives
when naked to naked goes.
I am shedding my garments one by one.

2.

THE RIMU TREE

Sprung from a lineage
of fantastical name,
you came
to this city park
almost a hundred years ago
from far away New Zealand,
gift of friendship to mark
the Panama
Pacific International
Exposition of 1918, an event
almost no one now alive
remembers
or cares about.

But you are still here,
unimaginably tall,
suffused with antique wisdom,
schooner's ancient mast
straining to reach the stars
you steer by.

You are like a willow
grown elegantly huge,
only you are a conifer
with braided leaves of
shadowed green
rough to the touch.
Your branches hang earthward
like that painter's well known scene
of a woman letting her hair down
to dry.

Without, you are beauty clarified

by time, shimmering jade
in the dappled light.
Inside you are a secret container,
a womb, a temple, a ceremonial tent,
a haven, a hidden sanctuary,
a cave,
a place to rest awhile
before starting out again.

3.

THE EPIPHANY

Old, broken off,
striated tree stump,
gleaming ash and gold
in the late afternoon sun--
I pause to marvel
at your hidden splendor.

Etched in your delicate folds
are whirls
like shells embracing,
or the undulant borders
of a palace painting
in Crete,
forgotten calligraphy
revealed by the shifting light,
waiting to be seen.

How lucky to arrive
at just this moment
and not some other.

4.

WHAT THE TULIPS SAID

(inspired by Louise Gluck)

Down here
where darkness thickens
in this tight sleeve of earth,
and filaments of root
run netted like a brain,
we have forgotten
about light,
the candles of the sun,
lost emblems of that other world.

Here our only occupation
is patience,
our sometime hope
the whispered news
that one day soon
all this will change
and we will be transmuted,
transposed to pure color--
scarlet, sapphire, gold--
flashing banners in the breeze,
hands stretched upward
signaling to those who pass,
see us,
what we have become,
this bright sensuousness,
unfurling edifice of joy.

THE HANG GLIDER

Graceful as any bird,
he flew across my horizon's sight
magnificent falcon in his ascent
until he passed before the sun
and disappeared
into that dazzling eye
and I, unwary, looked on and wondered
if he would, like Icarus,
plunge into the sea,
or else be swallowed up forever
in that implacable blaze.

But then his wings emerged again,
plunging and certain as before
and I looking earthward was left to gaze on
iridescent circlets of green
dancing across the even deeper green
of the ice plants glittering among the dunes,
and then the ocean turned relentless blue,
no, mercury colored, a cobalt mirror sheen
glinting, turbulent,
reflecting nothing at all,
and I wondered
was I blinded by the light
or had I at last reached final dark,
inscrutable embrace,
consumed by its tender,
unfathomable love.

DOLPHINS SPINNING

I saw them once,
the dolphins
spinning across our bow
off the coast of Florida
that day, so long ago.

And, for all I know,
they are still there,
welcoming the visitors,
circling the swimmers
in the water
like guides nudging
the water spirits home,
bringing their children
near the boat to show
that they too
are part of this world
of giving and breathing
and playing with seaweed
all day long,
its strands wreathing
their round faces
like necklaces
of the finest pearl,
like tokens of the grace
that comes to all of us
when we are there,
to witness.

KUNDALINI RETURNING
AT THE SEASIDE

Ah, well, old rover,
you've come back again.
Won't ask where you've been,
what company you've been keeping—
whether idling with some other tramp
ready and willing
then wondering what she has
let herself in for,
or else a pious type
praying all night for a sign
which finally comes,
moves in forever demanding ardor,
what then?

Whatever, I'm not jealous,
just glad you're home,
we wantons like
to take what comes,
and seize the day
whether it arrives
dressed in the latest look
or tattered rags,
summoned by some bar room tune,
or majestic concert in a hall.
As long as it is the familiar you.
As long as you knock and enter,
take up residence once again
as if you'd never left,
all promises and supplication
as before.

THE REBEL

Do not think
you are going to place me
in a barren cell
companioned only
with crucifix and straw,
hours of emptiness and fixed contemplation,
endless searching within,
as if I were in training to be a saint
or yet another savior of this stumbling world.

I will not answer
to your partitioned day,
your matins bell, sext and none,
nor meekly kneel when you come in
with your haughty crew
in their hanging gowns,
their dismissive way.

I reject your candles and perfumed soaked clouds,
your useless gestures
and incessant prayers
worn smooth by repetition,
all meaning gone.

This morning I went to the cliffs again
and gazed into
the toiling abyss below.
The sun flamed topaz gold
and the sea raged in ecstatic trance
an angry dakini,
Kali unleashed.

I waited. At last
she paused and bared
her naked breast
and sang her ancient song,
nuptial of heaven and unrepentant earth

There. At the edge.
Where beauty and terror meet.

THE TRUTH ABOUT CHAKRAS

Do not say,
This part is
animal,
that spiritual,
this one is higher,
that lower.
Quit trying to find new ways
to cut yourself in two.

When god made you
he blessed every part,
head, soles and everything
in between.

Then he kissed you again all over
as you were being born.

Now something lives within,
shy serpent self
who stirs and awakens only
from his constant need
to pierce,
to claim,
and let his hidden sweetness
overflow

THE SEA, THE SEA

Surefooted in their youth
they passed me on the narrow trail
above the cliff
and spoke in friendly, courteous tones
to me, respected elder,
and then moved swiftly on
to their appointed tryst
within the grove beyond,
whether a meeting of flesh
or spirit I did not know or care
as I watched their casual passage
along the treacherous path.

I, moving with greater caution,
had already, that day,
known the marriage bed
of sky and sea breeze,
sun and gulls sweeping forth
in their glittering arcs of air,
the ice plants swaying all the while,
translucent amethyst and gold,
together singing the bridal hymn of morning
as I trudged onward
in my joy.

POEMS FOR MARY OLIVER

1.

IN GRATITUDE

Because she was willing to do that,
because she was willing to step forth
and be the authentic being,
the true poet,

let the hawk's dark beak,
the bear's ravenous paw,
enter, become part of
who she was. . . .

She spent days
beside the pond
teeming with its watery life
of dragonflies
bits of darting light
stitching the surface
into a crisscross
of transparent fire,
the floating blooms
and the oddly engaging
amphibians
with their swollen bellies
and gaping mouths,
their raspy hellos—
who else could cherish these
in such measure?

Reckless nights in the woods
with its stealthy night prowlers
and haunting melodies

owl screech
and lonely night bird
chorus of snarls and growls
moving near
crackling underbrush
heavy falling limbs
oh, such sweet terror,
who knows what could have happened
there
in the center
of so much mystery. . . .

All of this
she sang in our ears,
gave to our awakening eyes,
as she became god's messenger,
the vessel to make us see.

2.

LIKE THE HIDDEN MOUNTAIN COLUMBINE

Is the soul solid like iron?
Or is it tender and breakable, like
the wings of a moth in the beak of the owl?
Mary Oliver

Is the spirit hard and impenetrable
like andradite or a chunk of fallen sky?
Or is it fluid like silt
at the bottom of a departed river,
or silk soothing the thighs
of an ancient dancer before the king?

Is it loud, like cymbals clashing
in front of a procession
heralding a hero's return . . . .
Or is it timorous and shy,
the notorious violet withdrawn
or the hidden mountain columbine . . . .

Does it go swaggering abroad daring the sunlight,
dazzling onlookers with its sheen,
or does it come creeping out at candlelight
furtively searching for the love it needs . . . .

This spirit, its cloak diaphanous or close woven,
how strange it is,
how enfolded in its
Mystery.

3.

MY WORK

My work is loving the world
Mary Oliver

I too have prized it
in all its intimacies.
its summer bloomings,
its nudities of winter.

Sometimes I sense a quiet
beneath the silence—
in the garden, perhaps,
the spreading hush
of the daffodils
and lilies,
or amidst those great trees
who have been here
for so long,
emissaries of the other realms,
saying, "peace, peace,
the world will endure
past all its losses."

Often it is the ocean itself
that speaks
in its roiling voice,
its thunderous tongue.

What it is saying
I have listened for
all these years.
as it crackles and whips,
or whispers in its silken tones.

Even now,
I am not sure of its message
its assaults of thrill and boom
shattering the rocks
into flares of light
something about Mystery,
something about uncontainable Love.

The Two Poets

Two sides of a coin,
twin masks mated forever,
the god who looks in different
directions
at once.

The earth's treasures,
the ocean flooding the marshes,
the shale,
the stars winking
their mysterious code,
the pelicans who come and go
with the seasons,
according to their need . . .

and the rain which washes
the faces of the flowers,
even the shyest buds . . .

one looks and exclaims
Oh yes, how beautiful!
the other murmurs
I mourn, I mourn.

AN ANGEL STRAYED INTO TIME*
(for Lisel Mueller)

Of the midwinter blooming,
she said it was
"out of phase, like an angel
strayed into time, our world."
And after listening to the concert
(Shubert by Brendel),
she felt she had for two hours
been in "the nowhere
where the enchanted live."

She herself prefers not to overstep,
not to be torn
by the storms of passion,
the earthquakes of revelation.

And so she flirts with it,
the delicate border
where the contraries meet,
this familiar sensed world
and that other, reputed realm
of the unqualified sublime
which beckons, like Avalon,
always just out of reach
in the mists of the never fully discerned.

By nature, a bit shy,
her language is her honed instrument
of exploration,
exposing the hidden unexpecteds
lurking in the midst of the usual.
Words measured, nuanced,
exact,

like a sudden small rainbow of light
which chooses to dance,
momentarily, over a flower
just about to open.

THE GIFTED POET
(for Louise Gluck)

I can do nothing but adore you.
Distantly. Without obtruding.

You peer forth from your death mask eyes,
with their sadness,
their grief filled resignation.

You have witnessed the world
in all its follies and
presumptions.
You know that things
do not endure.
You have seen the innocents rise
and fall again
into the thickening swamps
of oblivion.
You have borne it all stoically,
dedicated witness,
like a collector gathering specimens
for his catalogues of butterfly
or rock,
accepting each as it appeared,
withholding judgment.
You have raised your inner edifice
bit by bit of meticulous observation,
immaculate word piled
on immaculate word.
Nothing escapes you.

You maintain a careful distance.
Even touch, even acknowledgment,
is more than you can bear.

Your language shapes
a constantly flowing elegy
endless lament for the forsaken world,
continuous dirge for the lost self,
before the father vanished,
before the mother heaped on scorn,
and left only the frozen seer
whose polished words
became her essential armor,
her last defense
against a widening flood
of pain, a torrent of naked knowing.

BORGES IN HIS LABYRINTH*

*I am the one who never has unraveled
the labyrinth of time.*
Borges

This is the underside of faith,
the doubt which ever gnaws
at the solid bone of our belief.
We know it well,
our own once requisite shield of irony
and stoic resignation
before the anguish of incertitude.

He is the man poised
at the moment before illumination,
the blind man measuring his narrow walls
in quiet dignity,
cane tapping out the endless lengths of brick.
He is as well the prisoner
ascending the scaffold,
bound captive counting the moments
until the ax descends,
who stoically bares his nape
knowing he lives now in a world
where only the ax is real.

Transfixed, we watch his incessant circling,
his insistent pacing of the intricate maze
whose every fold and turning are now worn
smooth through his repeated touch.
We marvel at his graceful bearing
as he searches for the magic door
which will swing open, set him free.
Again, we whisper,
"Oh, Borges, if you only knew."

MARK DOTY

(Once during an acupuncture treatment, Mark
Doty, a brilliant writer of our time, experienced a
full blown mystical vision of the universe as an
infinite field of light. He chose not to pursue this
esoteric revelation, but to continue in his role as
artist and poet of the more tangible realities.)

This man has learned
to hedge his bets,
not to go too far,
stumble into those
fog ridden realms
where the mystics
and crackpots dwell.

His laser eyes
scan a provable landscape,
exposing unexpected vistas,
unguessed shadows.

His language is eloquent,
but he risks
only what is verifiable—
the scents and smells
of a summer day,
the revealed connections
of events and their origins,
pleasurable insights
into the hidden world
of a threaded reality
which startles but never stuns,
all well within the comfort zone
of our accepted possible.

His exquisite script
claims the world
as form,
thing seen anew
from a different angle,
something we covet,
yearn to hold close again.

LETTER TO ISSA*

Reflected
in the
dragonfly's eye . . .

mountains.

Issa (1763-1867)

Tell me, Issa,
what is a dragonfly's eye?

Is it a mirror
we walk through
each morning
to enter
our assumed world?

Is it a well
tunneling
into depths of darkness
and strangely lit hovering landscapes
we call our dwelling place?

Is it a map of our own features,
etched immutable
on a scarf of gold,
something to carry with us,
a reminder,
a talisman,
a conundrum daring us
to solve?

MUKUJIKI SHONIN

(This wood sculpture was part of an exhibit
displayed at the DeYoung Museum in San
Francisco, spring, 2006)

Mukujiki Shonin,
fat-faced Buddhist monk,
traveled village to village
carving tokens of his craft
(the village elders,
the waterfall)
even as he went.

This is his life-sized
self-portrait in wood
at 86,
round belly sagging
through his well worn gown,
smile with
twinkling eyes,
though his teeth are
no longer there
to prop his
sagging jowls.

How much misery
and grief
he must have met
along his way.
How much suffering
he must have witnessed
in that hostile world.

Yet he is still smiling
with his toothless grin.
How happy he seems.
How content he was
with all things,
as he patiently released
each image
from the waiting wood.

MONET

He was not afraid
of what was beautiful.

He was able to capture it,
place it on his canvas
like bits of colored light
frozen forever
into mosaic splendor.

The famous water lilies
were more than real,
beyond the merely observed.
Their chalices
leap from that shining surface
like lanterns set adrift
on water, to find their way
to other destinations,
regions not yet named.

And the cliffs, the winding
upward path, the trees and their
polished leaves,
you knew that you too had
been there,
breathed their brightness,
tasted those redolent hues
like strawberries
sweet and streaming
in the mouth.

You too felt the salted breeze
along the coastal shore,
your flesh stroked by the sensuous sun,
heard the surge and withdraw
of the deep sea drone,
the throaty note
from below.

What he gave us
was more than himself,
not just his eye, his craft,
but rather the thing itself,
the throb at the core.

Rothko

Something about the way
the paint moves
across the surface.

How the light strikes
the layers, the unfolding
path of the formless form.

How he poured
his soul (unproved)
into his work
like glaze.

Abandonment of the extraneous,
compression to source.

The invisible
struggling
to be seen,
before the waters and the land
were parted.

What energy possessed
this swimmer in the wine dark sea?
How did the brain ignite
and so surrender,
unveil
this forgotten knowing?

TO THE POET OF BOTH REALMS

(for Eric Ashford, who is the inspiration
of this poem and also the source of many
of its images.)

Somehow it did not occur to me
that She would come with a body.
Legs, hips, breasts and all the rest.
That you would paint that form
with a sheen of words,
tell of postures, motions,
the sounds that lovers make.

That you would brush your beloved's eyes
with kisses, leaving prints for the private
detectives of the soul to discover and
reclaim.

That you would build altars in
her hidden places,
and worship there.

That you would bring her gifts
of fire and water,
feed her the plunder of loam,
dazzle her with seeds of the sun.

You remind me of how it is to be enfleshed,
to go about in a temple made of light
and soft skin.

You whisper to your beloved,
who is sometimes palpable. like you,
sometimes is that Other, that invisible She
that we also know and sometimes seem to touch.

FOUR

MAKE LOVE YOUR BUSINESS

POEMS FOR MIRABAI

1.

THE BESOTTED FOLLOWER

To dance in this field
of radiance,
what will I give?

My good name, long since
taken from me.
My tattered robe,
with mud for its hem--
o, no, haven't seen it for days.
Family, friends—all have vanished,
have turned their faces away.

Still, I dance,
moving this way or that,
following the inner currents,
celebrating the hidden bliss,
my lone partner
Krishna and his silver flute,
that music which plays only for those
willing to be shattered
again and again,
ravished by sweetness,
torn by that joy.

2.

MORNING CHANT

I do not wish
to make something happen,
to force open
a gate or a window of bars
in order to find my way in.
All I want is to be
here with you,
the way it was last night.

Krishna, do not abandon me,
whatever comes.
I need you
in my blood and bones,
to feel your inner flowering
even when I wander,
lost in the meadows of thought.

You are the wild honey I crave,
the blue jewel
of radiance in my dreams,
the one who opens my eyes
each morning,
and says,
Behold, what loveliness this is.

3.

ONLY THIS

Out of it, you say,
See her, she is mad,
her sighs and curious movements,
her smile and absent gaze,
she is a lunatic lost
in an imagination gone astray.

This world and its occupations,
its priorities and needs,
these alone exist,
only these are real.

In it, you say,
This, yes this,
always without ceasing,
this is the only thing
I desire,
the single gift
I want.

MY TRIDENT AND BELL

I am willing
to go down.
I am willing to be
the crazed saint,
the raving mystic
babbling of god.

I am ready to invite
Shiva
into my bed.

Soon I shall cover
my body with ashes,
put a mark on my forehead,
go into the streets
with my trident
and bell.

You will not
know me then.
You will wonder
who I am,
what I am saying,
what became of the person
who used to live
at my former address.

PRACTICING THE AUSTERITIES

They have their
chakras and their nadis.

I have my living room bliss.

They arrange their bodies
in circles,
turn their legs into bent pins.

I stand quietly
letting the music streams
flow through.

They perform strange ablutions,
carefully measure what they eat.

Each day I brush my teeth
and shower, that's it.

Sometimes I even drink wine,
eat a bit of fish.

JADE GIRL, BLUE PHOENIX*

The jade girl sits
astride the blue phoenix.
They soar, upward,
into the golden eye of the sun.

She wears a translucent feather sheath.
It is soft as petals
falling on an improvised lake
quieted by storm.
Even the moon
riding the serene water
does not stir.

She has cultivated her inner richness,
her secret strength.
Like a woman warrior
who is clad beneath
in invisible armor of shells and forest bark,
nothing can deter her,
pierce her resolve.

Her thighs grip
the ascending bird.
A flash of indigo
streaks the sky.
He is taking her
where earth and heaven make love,
the forgotten place
where she has always been.

NIGHT AFTER NIGHT

Make love your business.
Rumi

I have made love
my business
and where has it
gotten me?

Nothing I would
care to share
with listeners.

Only this being
alone
night after night
with the Beloved,
faint with kisses.
It never ends.

A SHEEN OF SILVER

I do not know
whether to call you
my old dancer, or
my secret lover,
or maybe simply the One.

Like that bird who sang
outside my window
this morning,
was it an oriole or a robin
or some other,
more exotic breed. . . .
In the pale dawn
I couldn't tell for sure
as its song came
floating down
like a sheen of silver,
a proclamation of private joy,
as if it didn't care
what the rest of the world
thought of such insobriety,
whether or not we approved
of such unabashed display
in the midst of all
our concerns and worries.

And I listened content
though I still haven't
learned the names
of the many birds
or even the trees,
but then you don't have
to name things
in order to love them.

THEN ONE DAY

How can I know there is god
unless I feel it in my flesh?

For countless years
I read the books,
contemplated
the wise sayings.

Then one day
I was shocked by brilliance
and fell to my knees.

BREATHING LIGHT

This isn't the first time.

Being suffused
by unnamable love,
perfume from
an invisible rose.

I have long since
lost count,
given up trying
for useful definitions.

Description doesn't work
either.
The words are too small.

I am just glad
you came again,
showed up today.

MORE LOVE POEMS TO THE INVISIBLE

THIS GIFT

This gift you have given me
Who can say its value.
I can only clutch it
wait for something more.

***

How is it
that you keep returning. . . .
Even after the candle has
long since died away,
even when I have given up
the remains of my longing
and gone to dream
once more alone in my bed.

***

These words you keep slipping
into my mouth.
This throat kiss.
This terrible knowing
of what it is to be loved.

Nevertheless, I will keep returning,
Even if I still, after so many years,
do not know your name,
where you are coming from
how to follow you when you leave.

***

Now you are telling me
it doesn't really matter
how long this affair
has gone on,
when it began,
who made the first move.
You say this moment
is pure honey.
Drink.

ARE YOU WILLING!

The ascent to Joy
Is itself the transforming
Of fear into LOVE.
Marina Gamble

Are you willing to ascend to this joy?
It will tear you, rend you,
shatter your limbs
and fling them
into the sky
like dry sticks of straw
caught on the wind.

At times you will think you are drowning,
tossed in the furious ocean of longing,
at others,
that you are scorched
by unseen fires,
flare of passion.

Do you imagine you will
then remember who you are?
Why you began this journey?
Think well
before you enter this path.

Consider the price
of a single kiss.

WHATEVER THIS IS

What is it,
this channeling god,
these words pouring through
like love strokes of light,
these syllables taking over
becoming flesh, my flowing veins,
I cannot remember
when it was not this way,
when my blood did not ache
for whatever this is.

I SMILE BACK

I used to hide my words,
conceal them in a secret place,
a casket or an underground temple.

Now I flaunt them like jewels,
wear them like necklaces when
I take off all else
and go strolling through
the market square.

Some people see
my ornamented breasts
and smile,
others seem not to notice
or turn away.

I smile back at the smilers,
ignore the rest.

Perhaps someday they will
regain their sight.

SUFIS

Only yesterday I swore
to give up all this daylight
love play,
to get down to business,
early rising,
travel over rough trails,
brown bread and hard cheese
for lunch,
only water to drink.

But already this wisp of song,
these turning dancers
with skirts unfolding
like flowers awakened,
or birds spreading their white
or scarlet wings
in their flurry of ascent--
these have glazed my eyes,
carried me into
that other place,
secret trysting spot
familiar love ground. . . .

Sometimes I just stand here
thinking about you
and I disappear.

***

Listen, Listen...
Can you hear those honey drops fall
from the mouth of God?
Can you feel the rose
opening in your spine?
Whatever you were before

now you are only this.

***

Do you want
words
or feelings?
Or are they melted together like the love streaming
from your lover's eye
meeting the love
pouring from your own?

***

Does anyone else
feel this love?
Like the breath
of a thousand rose gardens
dreaming that they are petals
crushed in god's hand.

***

Is this from this world
or another . . . .
do these words have meanings
or are they mere love cries
from that one
come to kiss you awake again.
God has a thousand names
and I but one tongue
to tell them.

***

Some call me a wastrel,
some a wanton.
All I want
is to dance this dance
we do so well together.

***

Are you looking for the goddess?
She is
the lash on god's eye,
the hand stroking your velvet flesh alive,
the pearl
you found under your tongue
this morning.

***

All this time together
and still you have not told me
who I am,
where this journey leads.

TIME TO CONTINUE

Part of me saying,
enough, now I must rest
and then you answering,
no, time to continue,
forget about pauses,
no let up
for someone like you,
didn't you climb
into this honey bin
on your own,
try a few samples—
so go ahead, drown in this sweetness,
it is you.

IT REALLY WON'T MATTER

These inspirations,
these little beadlets of love,
who am I to refuse?

Yesterday,
you wanted sugared kisses.
Today love songs
in your ear.

Tell me who I am
and I will keep on singing
for you.
Or who you are
and I will begin
yet another poem.

Or don't say anything at all,
it really won't matter.
Even your silence
is beautiful.

HEAVY SECRETS

You and I
carry heavy secrets within.

This is why our breasts
have grown so large.

Already they are overflowing,
ready to fill
the world's waiting mouth.

YOUR OCEAN

(for Patricia)

Do you think such things
are not possible?
Have you looked in a mirror
lately,
seen the face you have become,
this sun marked visage,
this god shine parable
named you?

***

When you are in love
you do not say
you are near love
or beside love,
or seeking to know
love's truth.

You say you are in love.

Never mind how you got here.
This is your ocean.
Drown in it.

***

Now we are birthing
not just ourselves,
but the world and all its beings.

We are women squatting together
in a delivery circle,
bringing forth this new age,
this squalling,
wriggling time
ready to leap out,
shout its name aloud.

***

This canopy of words--
this outpour of sayings--
they help us to unlock
the glaciers of the mind,
unfurl the tight knit banners
waiting to proclaim presence,
capture us, make love.

***

Think about who you are.
Think of all that was rolled
into your skin
even before you were born.

What will you do with these gifts?
these sacraments waiting for you
to claim them.

TERESA IN ECSTASY

Bernini saw it.
Gave us
the woman in
her full inscrutable passion.

The angel stands near,
piercing her breast with his arrow,
lancing her heart
to love.

Nothing
in chapel or cell,
no soft telling of beads
or whispered hours
prepared her for this moment,
readied her for this time.

How, we wonder
can she abide
this fiery rapture,
relentless agony of ascent?

How endure
such final fusion,
this sudden annihilation
into light?

THE STAGES OF BLISS

Once, yogi returned,
I sat on the floor,
ankles crossed,
did puja with bells and clasped hands--
asanas were the key--
heavy bliss flows stirring
like rivers of love,
everything for the god/goddess
who had come at last.

Then I became music--
kirtans, bhajans,
Brahms,
honey in the throat,
the hands.
Sacred sounds
to stroke the hidden
centers awake,
angels
kissing me alive.
Who could refuse
such favor?

Then it was Buddha
beckoning,
thongka on my wall,
image bringing ineffable joy.
I bowed and rapture
flooded my crown,
my body.
I withstood it to the edge of feeling
as I rose toward some other realm.
Was I still there?

Now I stand
in the center of silence,
soft wind stirring leaves,
moon stilling the waters.
I bow quietly,
move little,
Light flowing
in gentle pulses,
a subtle sweetness,
the other telling me once more
who I am.

TRAVEL IN MY PALM

All the soothsayers
and astrologers
say I have travel
in my palm.

Yet I never
go anywhere
but here.

But this is where
it all takes place,
this going back and forth
between the realms.
Is this what they mean?

FIVE

LIVING WITH BUDDHA:

PROPHETS AND VOYAGERS,

SEERS AND SAINTS

THE GUIDES

Whoever you were,
you companioned me
from early on,
your words falling
into my ears
like drops of sweet oil
to sooth a child's complaint.

Always you took me
forward,
led me to wisdom books
where each page became
an open passage
through unexplored realms:
revelations lurked
like exotic species,
strange animals peering
from tropical darkness.

Now your whispered truths
have merged into my cells,
become how I see the
things around me . . .
the bent tree bowing to heaven,
the bee hovering,
ready to make love to
its waiting paramour,
the scarlet bird caught against
the anguish
of the whitening sky.

And always,
the unsayable bliss
when you appear.

VASUGUPTA*

was my uncle,
a great and holy man,
he let the gods speak
through his lips,
their words of wisdom
also seen on rocks
and mountains,
all the workings of the inner
and the outer worlds
his to convey.

I was sent to him most early,
a child instructed
by a wizened priest.
He taught me how to sing
the notes and intonations,
how to forget all else
and let the sacred voice
echo in my mouth,
the presence dwell inside my heart.

Mine were not the gifts
of that great man,
the rishi-being Vasugupta
destiny's vessel,
yet my voice was clear.
I had my place of honor
among the singers.
I lived a long and wholesome life
and died with music
in my throat.

WHAT THE GODS REQUIRE:
THE PROPHET

(for Andrew)

They want you as their
sacrifice.

The lamb that lies down,
full of arrows,
roses blooming scarlet
at every opening.

They want you to speak endlessly,
your mouth, your throat
an instrument for that
which is hidden, has never been
said.

They want you to be available.
Time is short.

They want you to be forgetful
of everything that went before,
even your triumphs and accolades,
your ribbons of celebration.

They want you to continue forever,
like a pure ray of light
extending into the unseen infinite,
which does not bend, nor remember
its beginnings,
nor even when it passed over
into that other realm.

THE ANCIENT SEER INVOKES
THE UNSEEN POWERS

*Some days, it is easier to commune
with gods than others.*

Normandie Ellis,
Awakening Osiris

I wish to say words
which have never been written.
I wish to speak
with all the invisible ones,
those who surround me,
so that our voices may swell
into a chorus of sounding.
I wish to steal the eye
of Horus,
to place it in my head,
so that I may see others
as they are,
skeletons of light
moving about earth.
I wish to hear
with the ear
of Horus, that I
may grasp the spokenness
of secrets, the saying
of what is hidden.
I wish to fly
high over the earth,
to trace with my seeing
the lacy nets of rivers,
like trees flattened, sending
their curving fingers through sand,
through fields of green.

I wish to descend,
to become a jewel, a jasper
hidden in the dark thighs of earth.
I wish to float through the mouths
of men bearing loads of wood
for the cooking fires,
of women waking their babes
for the morning breast.
I wish to enter
the words of a sacred script,
to be that which the priestess allows
to come forth, energy
of the very source of creation,
text filled with secret power.
I wish to worship in temples
with fire and incense,
to an unknown god.
I wish to move with whales through
dark water, deep
in the flowery veins of ocean.
I wish to be still,
to wait with the
watchers gathering to see the sun
stain the sky
with dawn, to crimson the earth
with morning fire.
I wish to know who I am,
the hidden one come forth
like a fruit of
an ancient tree.
I wish to find my others,
those who with me form
a constant being.
I wish to be made strong,
in order to bear secrets.
I wish to be shaped

into smoothness,
that I may bear
love.
I wish to hear
the word unspoken,
the syllable of god.
Help me to fling down
my knowledge
before the feet of
the gods, to pare away
my learning like
the skin of an apple.
Let me strip off my clothes,
my skin, the outer part of my membranes
and coverings,
my bones, my organs of living,
let me become
a nothingness,
an invisible seed
at the center,
the core of that
which does not exist.

THE ORACLE AT DELPHI

I don't know what to do
but to say what I must say,
to know what I know.

The earth here is unsteady,
trembling as if to warn.

I have gone through many disasters,
seen the empires rise and fall.

The celebrated ones come
from afar with tribute,
eager to learn their fate,
who will be victorious,
who will not survive.

That was before everything shifted,
remnants could be salvaged
from the ruins.

What should I tell them now?
Are they ready to hear?

Already there is
echoing in the earth,
the seas are swaying,

Who is prepared
to listen,
strong enough to bear
the words I bring. . . .

IN THE MIDST OF FALLING

(In ancient Egypt, the mouth of the deceased—who
was now dressed in mummy cloth—was "opened" as
part of the ritual of reawakening as a divinity.)

Oh, it is time, it is time,
to give the gods
mouths to sing.

Though our world is dissolving around us
like bits of dust in water
still, now is the time,
the inevitable time,
the necessary moment
for the gods to sing.

All around us is departure, a going away.
Nothing remains in its rightful place.

The mothers, the grandmothers
all are disappearing
or wandering the world
seeking their lost children.
The sons and the fathers
have vanished long ago.

Yet, even now, in the midst of the falling,
the desolation and the cries,
the gods are rousing,
opening their mouths,
soon to sing.

THE RISHIS

What they knew
was that life
is not a pure exposition
of darkness, or light,
but a compendium,
a constantly shifting
blend,
as if from a master of chiaroscuro
who wanted to try all
the possible combinations
and angles,
gradations and permutations
of depiction
before declaring balance,
and then not stasis,
but the delicate harmony
of chaos, where everything streams,
each shifting molecule,
each flowing strand of transitoriness
straining toward fulfillment,
not through blatant symmetry
but from the hidden skein
of a tangled, crafty design.

FINALLY WE TOOK AN AX

For years we circled
our hidden chamber,
seeking a way out.

Nothing sufficed:
Not prayers,
nor supplications,
not knees against stone,
nor heavy penance
of nails and shirts of hair.

Finally, we took an ax
and broke through to god.
At first we were blinded by the splendor,
the majesty and
shining raiment.
We crept closer
and raised our head a little.

That one said,
where have you been,
my dear one?
I have been waiting for you
for so many years.

BURNING CLAY

It is almost like this:
a code, a waiting key,
perhaps a still tone
awakening the within.

To step now
into arms of darkness,
to open to what awaits,
the love, the fury,
command and echo,
summoning
and release.

Something about lifetimes
of getting ready,
the voice from a past
lost forever in cycles of light,
cones of burning clay.

What will you give for this?
What will you give?

ONLY WHAT DANCES

I transgress.

Lord, join me in these fields of love.

I stand always
outside the gates,
beneath the walls
of the bastioned city.

Lord, join me in these fields of love.

I am the one
they warn
the young ones against,
the daughters
who come to me
at twilight
bearing gifts.

Lord, join me in these fields of love.

When the sun
breaks over the distant hills,
my music floats
over cypress and pine.
My call echoes
across the snowy peaks,
the hidden valleys.

Lord, join me now in these fields of love.

The planets pulse
with the breath of my being,
the distant stars float by

in ecstasies of sound,
my rhythms foretell
the rise and fall of
dominions and heavenly bodies.

Lord, you who are as well my Lady,
come to me now,
let us move together.
Only what dances is real.

LIKE FLOWERS THAT BLOOM AT MIDNIGHT

I know all about
living in caves
with candles and scented prayers,
crossing the desert which never ends
seeking the One who is always near,
spreading my deerskin
in the forest depths
where the spirits of the blue bodied gods
hang like shadows of watching birds.

With the others, I wove
a story of connection,
something mysterious and inscrutable
we called to appear
with our fires and recitations
our songs of supplication and praise . . .
a voice spoke through us
as we chanted our words
and the centuries passed.

This time I came in other guise.
I roamed the avenues,
mingled in the market
with the restless crowds,
watched and listened in alarm
as the world reeled and
spun down
toward its approaching dark.

.

And I saw that this
was the time
to take on new knowledge,
move through different space,
hear with unfamiliar ears,
speak with strengthened voice,
atoms transfigured,
senses restrung,
it is happening to us all,
blazing illumination,
beauty erupting in the midst of despair,
splendor unveiled
on a field of pain,
we are being filled with light
we do not comprehend
lifted toward essence
assaulted by nameless love
at this juncture
of the finalities,
intersection of the unimaginables . . .
this is why we came.

LIVING WITH BUDDHA

(Recently I purchased a Buddhist thongka
which seems to possess special powers of
awakening the inner vibrations. This
poem is about this experience.)

1.

I never expected this.
As always, it was just the music and me,
the vibrations coming on like waves
ruffling the shore.
And then the Unseen came,
taking my breath,
sly cat circling the cradle
where the naked baby lies,
and suddenly—
You appeared,
radiant being
lit from within
like an icon set in a temple
incandescence lighting
your face, your breast,
now there was the outer image,
and this inner brightness as well--
what was I to do?

2.

True, there had been a time of preparation, a
leading up—
for days, Tibetan music
with its raucous gongs and drums
beating the blood
to a kind of inner frenzy,

slow movement whipping the vibrations
to a pitch,
like a lash
over the waves,
everything pulsating,
bliss, they call it,
who can give it a name?

3.

And then the day when many Buddhas
came within
in geometric procession,
appearing one behind the other,
like figures in a text
on perspective,
showing how objects maintain power
even as they diminish,
I couldn't even move.

4.

I found it there days earlier,
on the wall of the import store,
holding me in its gaze,
Buddha in a wall painting,
a kind of scroll
with the Teacher
captured in the design,
they name it a thongka,
majestic presence
calling me.

But I didn't yield.
I left empty handed.

5.

But later
I returned,
telling myself,
If it's still there,
I'll take it,
if not, I'll simply say
it wasn't meant to be,
and muse on nonattachment.

It was waiting.
I ran my hand over the face
and felt sweetness
ripple like musk-scented breezes
over my wrist.
I'll take it, I said.

6.

Next morning,
when I bowed
to this image
on my wall,
the energies
pulsed so sweet and strong
I almost could not stand.

First, my head
was blessed
as if his aura
touched my own,
then torso, legs,
arms and hands
all began quietly to move,
to slowly dance,

and I became a turning
Buddha field
of light,
my limbs like blossomings of
love,
some kind of nectar,
I could not even ask
what was happening,
I could only
become
whatever it was.

7.

And so each morning,
there was boundless bliss
and inner teachers came,
each day someone new,
I gave them nicknames
to keep them straight,
"Sturdy Boy" or "Master Chi"
or "Ting Mao" with his flowing
sleeves and fan,
Tara with my mother's face,
so many, all to lead me
in my morning rite,
new movements, new postures,
I was easily led, bliss currents streaming.

8.

When I moved in close
to get a better look,
the Buddha field
surrounded me.
I turned my face gently

right and left,
I felt its soft stroke
along my cheeks,
I bowed
and began my movements
once again.

How many minutes
could I stay
in this electric clasp?
How long survive
in this dense
torrent of love?

9.

High, high.

Were these the vibrations
of the outer realms,
the place of gods and
deities of every kind,
the supramundane,
suprahuman,
other worldly
spirits from the
secret spheres.

When Zeus came down to Semele,
she vanished in a flash.

Who can withstand
such all devouring love,
who is willing
to be pierced again and again by light,

light purified at source?

First, you arrived
like a flower
lit from within,
holding its own sun.

I let your
multiple form
inhabit my mind.

Now you are an image
poised
against my wall.

Each morning
I stand before you, bow,
move about a bit,
while you watch quietly
in your steady pose,
you the unchanging,
compassionate wisdom,
easy love.

WHO WOULD HAVE LISTENED?

It wasn't enough
that it happened,
that our bodies
were torn
by a joy so
deep it
could not be translated,
not even a Biblical
utterance
could have captured
an event
of such proportions,
so rare
as to be
indefinable,
there was no one
to listen,
and besides,
who would have believed
such a story,
so unlikely,
improbable,
like a myth
or a hero's false tale?

I WILL

If you want me
to fling myself in,
yes, I will do that,
this fire does not burn.

If you want me to linger
along the edges,
in a stance of contemplation,
probing the Mystery--
oh, what does it mean?

If you want me to
speak to multitudes,
to utter
your hidden syllables
to masses of hearers,
I will clear my throat
and begin.

If you want me to be still,
say nothing,
eyes shut to all
but where the radiant
darkness dwells,
I will open my heart
to silence,
let my spirit
swell with compassion,
become love.

ON ONE SIDE

On one side of the path, ecstasy,
on the other, dull grief...
Denise Levertov

Hail to the mother of us all!
I salute the holy receptacle
from which we come!
Anonymous

I slip through
the narrow opening
between the great rocks
which witness
in silence.

I continue,
into sun,
into darkness,
sometimes stumbling,
sometimes plunging ahead.

At night
I slumber
beside my fire
as the eyes of the beasts
stare back at me,
red embers flaring from
the veil of dark.

By day, the sun
emblazons the wavering landscape,
burning fields of amber light,
forests ringed
by fire.

I have forgotten about food.
I drink the dew of the leaves
at morning,
find hidden springs
beneath the stones.

I continue
for countless unmarked hours,
innumerable streaming days,
sometimes forgetting
that this path is mine,
the one
I have chosen,
the way I have wanted
to be.

I will know
my destination
when I arrive.

Notes

"An Angel Strayed into Time" : This poem is dedicated to Lisel Mueller, one of the finest poets of our time, whose delicate sensibility has been a great gift to all of us. She speaks with consummate artistry about the human condition.

"The Gifted Poet" : This is for Louise Gluck, whose exquisite verses reveal, always, an elegant truth. Through the alchemy of her work, she transmutes suffering into beauty.

"Borges in His Labyrinth": Jorge Luis Borges is acclaimed as one of the greatest writers of the twentieth century. He typifies the contemporary intellectual whose vision is comprehensive, but who cannot escape the prison of the mind to enter the states of full mystical illumination and transcendence. The labyrinth was one of his favorite metaphors to describe his condition as thwarted seeker.

"Jade Girl, Blue Phoenix" : The title and opening image are taken from *Immortal Sisters*, ed. Thomas Cleary

"Vasugupta": Vasugupta was a ninth-century sage of the Kashmiri Shaivite tradition (followers of Shiva who originally lived in Kashmir.) He is credited with writing the basic texts of the Shiva-Sutras, which were revealed to him through divine inspiration. This channeled poem is meant to be chanted in a sing-song monotone.

157

Dorothy Walters, Ph. D., lives and writes in San Francisco. She was for many years a professor of English and Women's Studies in a Midwestern university. In 1981, she experienced a major kundalini awakening, and the rest of her life has been shaped by this profound spiritual experience, which continues to unfold.. She has published two books relating to spiritual transformation : *Marrow of Flame*: *Poems of* the *Spiritual Journey* (available from Amazon and Hohm Press) and *Unmasking the Rose*: *A Record of a Kundalini Initiation* (e-mail Dorothy for this book, formerly from Hampton Roads.) Her poems and prose reflections have appeared in several anthologies of spiritual writings, as well as journals and other publications.

Dorothy is available for poetry readings and other presentations relating to mystical awareness, particularly experiences of kundalini awakening. She offers a blog at www.kundalinisplendor.blogspot.com (Poems and Reflections on the Spiritual Journey).

Like many others, she believes that kundalini is a manifestation of the divine reality, and is the instrument by which humanity will progress to the next stage of spiritual and psychological evolution

Dorothy may be reached at: dorothywalters2@sbcgobal.net She is happy to answer questions relating to kundalini , and to hear from readers who themselves are undergoing deep spiritual transformation.